**W9-BNG-773**

# GERYON

# MONSTERS OF MYTHOLOGY

## 25 VOLUMES

### Hellenic

Amycus
Anteus
The Calydonian Boar
Cerberus
Chimaera
The Cyclopes
The Dragon of Boeotia
The Furies
Geryon
Harpalyce
Hecate
The Hydra
Ladon
Medusa
The Minotaur
The Nemean Lion
Procrustes
Scylla and Charybdis
The Sirens
The Spear-birds
The Sphinx

### Norse

Fafnir
Fenris

### Celtic

Drabne of Dole
Pig's Ploughman

MONSTERS OF MYTHOLOGY

# GERYON

*Bernard Evslin*

**CHELSEA HOUSE PUBLISHERS**

New York     Philadelphia

1987

**EDITOR**
Jennifer Caldwell

**ART DIRECTOR**
Giannella Garrett

**PICTURE RESEARCHER**
Susan Quist

**DESIGNER**
Victoria Tomaselli

**CREATIVE DIRECTOR**
Harold Steinberg

3  5  7  9  8  6  4  2

Library of Congress Cataloging-in-Publication Data

Evslin, Bernard.
Geryon.

(Monsters of mythology)
Summary: Recounts the classical myth about
the triple-bodied monster who lost his life
and herd of red oxen in a battle with Hercules.
1. Geryon (Classical mythology)—Juvenile
literature. [1. Geryon (Classical mythology)
2. Hercules (Roman mythology) 3. Mythology, Classical]
I. Title. II. Series: Evslin, Bernard. Monsters of
mythology.
BL820.G47E97      1987      398.2'454'0938      87-8033

ISBN 1-55546-250-2

Printed in Singapore

For my grandson
NATHANIEL EVSLIN
who is less a monster than any child I've ever met.

# Characters

## Monsters

| | |
|---|---|
| **Geryon**<br>(GUR ih uhn) | A three-bodied monster; also known as the Triple Terror of Thessaly |
| **Snapping turtle, Sickle-fish, and Whip-snake** | The appropriated forms of the river god Castelos |
| **Giant shark** | An ordinary fish, magically enlarged |

## Gods

| | |
|---|---|
| **Castelos**<br>(KAS tell uhs) | A river god; father of Calliroa |
| **Atropos**<br>(AT roh pohs) | Eldest of the Fates; Lady of the Shears; she cuts the thread of life |
| **Lachesis**<br>(LAK ee sihs) | The second Fate; she measures the thread of life |
| **Clotho**<br>(KLOH thoh) | Youngest of the Fates; she spins the thread of life |

| **Hera**<br>(HEE ruh) | Queen of the Gods |
|---|---|
| **Ares**<br>(AIR eez) | God of War |
| **Poseidon**<br>(poh SY duhn) | God of the Sea |

## Demigods

| **Calliroa**<br>(kuh LIHR ruh) | A river nymph; daughter of Castelos and mother of Geryon |
|---|---|
| **Hercules**<br>(HER ku leez) | Son of Zeus; the greatest hero of ancient times |

## Others

| **Giant bats** | The guise of the Three Fates |
|---|---|
| **Suitors** | Those who come to woo Calliroa |
| **Pygmies** | A colony of little people on the river Nile |
| **Tattle-bird** | Hera's spy |
| **Hundred-handed Giants** | Hera's servants |
| **Slaves** | Those who serve Geryon |

# Contents

# 1

## The Three Fates

Of all the monsters who sought to destroy Hercules, the most dreadful, perhaps, was the three-bodied Geryon, also known as the Triple Terror of Thessaly. This tale has deep roots; its seeds were planted long before Geryon was born, in the very year that the dawn-hero, Perseus, was stalking the snake-haired Medusa.

It all began one windy night in a cave on the western slope of Olympus, where dwelt three ancient sisters known as the Fates. Atropos, the Scissors Hag, was ranting at her sisters, raising her voice above the screech of the wind:

"We have enemies, I tell you!"

"Who dares challenge us?" yelped Lachesis.

"Yes, sister, who, who?" howled Clotho.

"Stop hooting like an owl," said Atropos, "and listen. A new breed has arisen among humankind, a select few who seek to blur the designs of destiny. Instead of worshiping the official gods and meekly obeying our edicts, they intend to follow the arch-meddler, Prometheus, who defied us by giving man the gift of fire."

"Who are these troublemakers, who, who?"

"They are called heroes," said Atropos. "They move restlessly from adventure to adventure, upsetting the natural order, breaking the webs of fate we so carefully spin."

"How?" asked Lachesis. "What do they do?"

"Different things, all of them troublesome. They're either brawling young brutes like Hercules and Perseus, who go about killing monsters who should be killing them. Or they're pesky questioners who keep poking their noses into our most sacred arrangements, always asking 'How does it work? How can it be changed? Why, why?' And then there's the sneaky, gentle kind like Asclepius, who dares to overturn our dooms, dosing people with his damned herbs, sewing up wounds, resetting bones, pulling his patients from the very brink of death and robbing our cousin Hades of his proper quota of corpses."

"Makes you think, doesn't it?" murmured Lachesis. She was the one who measured the thread that Clotho spun and Atropos cut. This was the Thread of Life, out of which the three sisters wove the web of Fate. Each time Atropos cut the thread it meant death.

"Yes," said Clotho. "Her words are full of wisdom; they do make one think. And thinking makes one thirsty, very thirsty." She dipped a ladle into the great vat of barley beer that stood near the hearth; the other sisters dipped their ladles too, and drank deep. They were gluttons. As ancient as they were, they had kept their big yellow teeth and could crack marrow bones, something they did all day long and much of the night. The sisters sat down to regular meals, of course, but they also ate while they worked. Nor did they foul their webs, for they kept curly-headed slaves to wipe their greasy fingers on.

"Thinking makes one thirsty," muttered Lachesis. "And drinking makes one hungry."

"But you never speak idly, sister," said Clotho. "An intention always lurks behind your words. What do you want us to do—reinforce our webs so that these heroes can't escape their fates?"

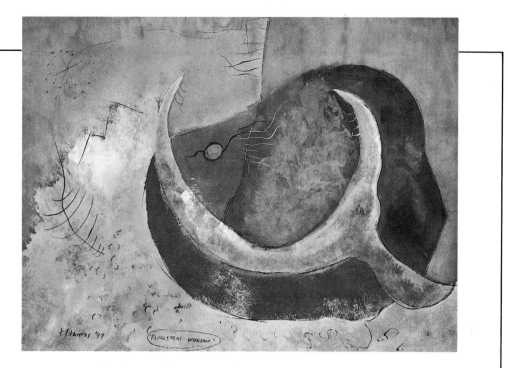

*Each time Atropos cut the thread it meant death.*

"By all means," said Atropos. "We should do that. But we must do more, I'm afraid. We must leave our cozy home and go on an inspection trip to see just what these pesky heroes are up to. Then we'll be able to patch our webs more precisely."

"Oh dear," said Lachesis. "I hate to travel. It's a sorry business. Can't eat properly on the road."

"As it happens, we can do two things at once," said Atropos. "A place I particularly want to visit is the western shore of the River Castelos, where great events are fated to transpire. We must look over that ground carefully. There's an oak grove near the river whose acorns are very fat and flavorsome. And the wild pigs who eat these acorns are also very fat and flavorsome. The flesh of their suckling pigs is said to be of unparalleled flavor."

The sisters slavered as they heard these words. Roast piglet was their favorite dish.

"Yes," said Atropos. "We'll round up a nice batch of these sucklings and bring them back with us. That should make up for the discomforts of travel."

# 2

## Bats on the River Bank

The three sisters changed themselves into bats for their journey, giant bats, who slept by day and flew at night. When they flew low their wingspread blotted the moon. They flew here and there, spying on people—on kings and slaves, heroes and cowards, lovers and killers, and many who were none of these things but simply lived as they could, hoping to avoid trouble and keep going from day to day.

On the last night before returning home, the sisters alighted on the shore of the River Castelos, where they hoped to catch suckling pigs, enough to last them through the winter.

Now, the local river god who had given his name to these waters was someone very hard to get along with. He had a savage temper. He hated strangers—almost as much as he despised acquaintances. Boasting the purest waters in all the land, he drove away any animals that tried to hunt along his shores, for he couldn't bear the idea of blood seeping into his river. The only creature in the world he didn't hate was his beautiful naiad daughter, Calliroa. Nevertheless, he had always wished that she were a boy. For he dreaded the prospect of her marrying someone someday; he knew he would hate her husband, whoever he was.

Particularly loathsome to Castelos were bats. His waters were fed by icy little springs born out of the winter snows, which turned into boisterous streams as they tumbled down the mountain slopes. These streams ran through caves and under rock walls where bats clung. They hung like rags from the ceilings of the caves until nightfall when they suddenly became winged rats with terrible claws, who hunted through the night, killing everything they could catch and drinking its blood.

Upon this night, the moon knelt low and burned so brightly that it was like a muted sun, strong enough to cast shadows. Castelos and his daughter rose from the spangled river to bathe themselves in golden light.

Something darkened the moon. The naiad uttered a half cry. Castelos saw the shadow of wings branding his shores— huge wings, not tapered but fan-shaped and strangely ribbed. Three enormous bats were settling upon the riverbank. The god had seen enough. He grasped his daughter's arm and pulled her under the water.

"What are they, father?" she cried. "Are they bats? They're so big!"

"Stay here," he said. "I'll get rid of them."

He pushed her into the underwater cave where they dwelt, and began to stir his river into a flood. So enraged was he at the sight of the loathsome creatures that he didn't even bother to surface for another look. He didn't see the bats strip off their wings like capes, twitch their rat faces back into crone faces, and stand revealed as themselves, the Three Hags of Fate.

Tittering and chuckling in the moonlight, they began to caper with excitement, for they smelled suckling pig on the wind.

But the hags were given no chance to hunt. Castelos was busy below, and the river swelled with his rage. It rushed, it foamed, it overflowed its banks in a mighty spate and swept over the land, washing away everything that stood before it, including the three sisters. Being immortal, they couldn't drown, but they could suffer discomfort.

Now, gathering their wet cloaks about them, they bobbed on the surface, shivering, and clinging to one another. Castelos rose from the river and saw a seething waste of waters. He studied the treeline and the sky, saw no bats flying against the moon, and laughed to himself. He raised both arms high and whistled loudly, summoning the waters to subside. Obediently, they shrank back between their banks.

Then, Castelos froze with horror. The bats had returned; they had sprouted legs, and were dancing about waving their wings and screeching at him. Their hag voices were like knives slashing away at his power, letting his strength drain out, and fear enter. They screeched:

*His waters were fed by icy little*
*springs born out of the winter snows.*

*"We Hags of Fate know how to hate,*
*and whom to curse with magical verse."*

River, take care,
River, beware.
Rolled in mud
by your insolent flood,
we Hags of Fate
know how to hate,
and whom to curse
with magical verse.

River, take care,
River, beware.
Monsters three
shall your daughter bear.

They shall hunt
along your shore,
killing, killing,
spilling gore,
fouling your waters
forever more.

The hags uttered the last mighty rhyme of their curse, spread their cloaks and flew off, still screeching.

For the first time in his life, Castelos was afraid. Before this, the only fear he had known was the fear he had caused. For in those days, people who dwelt in delta lands were affected by the whims of their local river god far more than by any of the distant gods of Olympus. Their lives literally hung on the antics of the river, which in flood swept away houses and barns and those who lived in them, and buried fields under tons of water. At other times, the river simply shrank itself into a miserly muddy trickle, leaving crops to wither on the stalk, cattle to thirst, and people to starve.

Thus it was that up till now, Castelos had spread fear but had never felt it himself. Now everything had changed. The giant bats had blotted the moon and settled loathsomely on his bank. When he had tried to drown them, as was his right, they had changed into the very Hags of Fate, cursing him forever, and naming his daughter as both the victim and the instrument of their vengeance.

# 3

# The Suitors

espite all the magical verses and moonlit curses uttered by all the capering hags in the world, Castelos was not one to acquiesce in his own doom. He said to himself, "If I arrange matters so that no male of any species is able to approach my daughter, then she will bear no child—singleton, twin, or triplet—monster, or otherwise. I shall keep her strictly secluded, and in my behavior shall set an example for suspicious fathers everywhere."

Now, Calliroa was very shy, appearing only after sunset and before dawn to dive off rocks and play with the swans. Nevertheless, she had been seen, and young men came courting. Nor were they discouraged by rumor that her father was an ogre who had promised death to all who wooed her. Such rumors only made the idea of winning her more attractive. For in the springtide of life when youth is maddened by unspent energy, danger adds spice to any possibility. It is so now, and was even more so then, when the entire human race was in its springtime.

So the young men came courting, and some that were not so young—warriors, captains, princes, a widowed king or two. They appeared on the shore at all hours, some with rich gifts, calling into the waters. They spoke to her in various ways:

"Nymph. Maiden. River's daughter. Come out! Come out! Come see what I have brought you! Come be my bride!"

But not one of them was given time to press his suit, for Castelos was there, crouching underwater on mighty legs, waiting to attack.

A young poet who came at the first light of dawn was rewarded by the sight of Calliroa completing her last dive. He caught a searing glimpse of her long legs entering the water and was so excited that he hopped up and down on the shore, shouting: "Nymph! Nymph! Come out! Please come out. I can't go in after you; I'll drown."

A column of mist rose from the river and thickened before his wondering eyes. It congealed into the shape of a gigantic snapping turtle. The youth gaped in amazement.

*The young men came courting. . . .*
*They appeared on the shore at*
*all hours, calling into the waters.*

"Begone," said the turtle in a throaty voice. "You stand upon a fatal shore. Depart, or die."

"Thank you for your warning, good turtle," said the young man courteously. "But I cannot leave just yet. For I have fallen in love with the nymph who dwells in this river. And I mean to marry her."

The turtle did not reply. It simply tucked in its head and legs and spun out of the water like a discus. It skidded to a landing on the shore, poked out its leathery head and advanced on the boy. He was too poor to own a sword. All he carried was his lyre, slung over his shoulder, and a wooden staff. He felt very frightened as the huge turtle came toward him, but was determined not to be chased away. He clutched his staff and prepared to strike.

"Stop where you are," he said. And was disgusted to hear his voice quavering. "Stop right there or I'll smash your shell with my stick."

The turtle lunged. The youth struck. The turtle caught the staff in his jaws and snapped it in two like a twig. The lad realized that those terrible jaws could break an arm or leg just as easily. He whirled and ran away as fast as he could, hating himself for his cowardice. He didn't stop running until he reached the top of a hill, and the river was just a silver thread far below. There he sat on a rock and wept. "I shall never forget her," he vowed. "I shall spend the rest of my life making verses about nothing but her, her, her!"

Indeed, for some weeks he did go about muttering passionately to himself about the nymph he had seen diving through the pearly light of dawn. He kept grieving in verse until he met an oak dryad who had no jealous father and who taught him to forget the river nymph. He never forgot the giant turtle, though, and for the rest of his life avoided rivers and streams and bathed only when he was caught in the rain.

The next suitor came to the river at noon. He was no fragile poet but a big, burly young man wearing breastplate and helmet, bearing sword and shield. He beat sword against shield, making a great clamor, and shouted, "Naiad! Naiad! Naiad!"

A spout of mist rose from the water. It thickened into the shape of an enormous fish, but such a one as the suitor had never seen. A horn grew out of its head, a long curved ivory blade, and the suitor realized that he was looking upon the sickle-fish, a creature most rare, of which dreadful tales were told.

Hanging in its column of mist, the fish slithered toward a willow tree that grew on the shore, its boughs dipping gracefully toward the water like a maiden washing her hair. The fish flailed its body; the ivory blade sheared the willow branches as neatly as a scythe. The boughs fell into the water and slowly floated away as the young man stared in amazement.

But he did not run. He never ran before an enemy. Instead, he about-faced and marched off—firmly, but not too slowly. He didn't look back. It was an orderly retreat, and he never returned.

For other, more dangerous-looking suitors—and there were many who courted his daughter—Castelos put on the third and most deadly of his transformations. He would rise from his depths as a whip-snake—a hundred yards of living muscle, encased in sliding leather scales, tougher than bronze, and edged along its entire length by a murderous ridge of spines. In this form Castelos could hover over an entire troop of armed men. He would crack his body like a bullwhip and simply sweep the phalanx away, crushing them like beetles in their armor. If a princely suitor survived the massacre of his royal guard, he would run for his life, vowing to forget river nymphs and marry the rich, ugly princess his mother had chosen for him.

Some powerful princes, however, came even more heavily escorted. They arrived with squadrons of battle-trained spearmen and archers, who stationed themselves on both sides of the river, ready to destroy anything that threatened their leader. For such suitors Castelos would forego his transformations. No giant snapping turtle, no sickle-fish, no whip-snake would appear from the river, but the river itself would rise.

Castelos would crouch in the depths, stirring, making the river swell higher and higher until it overflowed its banks and rolled across the fields in a seething brown flood, sweeping away everything that stood in its path, drowning every living creature that did not flee to high ground. Only when the countryside had been swept bare of anything that might call itself a suitor did Castelos recall the waters.

Thus it was that Castelos kept his daughter from marriage. "I've stopped those rancid old hags in their tracks," he muttered to himself. "No three monster grandsons shall I have hunting along my shores and fouling my waters with the blood of their kill. Yes, I've thwarted the Fates so far and must continue to do so."

But for all his self-con-gratulation, Castelos did not permit himself to get befuddled by success. He kept his wits, kept studying the situation. He knew that boys and girls who wanted to meet each other became more slippery than eels and managed to elude the strictest parental vigil. He remembered how a king of a nearby country had sought to thwart a prophecy that he would be killed by his own grandson. He had imprisoned his only daughter in a doorless, windowless brass tower, and thought he had found a foolproof way to keep suitors out—until, one day, passing the tower, he heard the sound he dreaded most—a baby's cry. He ordered his slaves to break down the walls of the tower and found his daughter seated calmly amid the rubble nursing a day-old child. She informed her father that the babe was sired by a god who pierced the tower as a shaft of light. The boy did indeed grow up to kill his grandfather, accidentally, it was claimed, but sufficiently to fulfill the prophecy.

"So . . . " muttered Castelos to himself. "It is not enough to drive away suitors, which I'm getting very good at. I must stop her from even thinking about marriage and children. I'll have to find a way to make her put these things out of her mind forever."

Several days passed. The river god was in the great underwater cave that formed his palace. Clad in his royal cloak of crocodile hide, wearing his opal crown, he sat on a rock that made a natural throne. His daughter, Calliroa, knelt at his feet, threading periwinkle shells into tiny necklaces for her family of dolls. Although tall and ripe, she was still childish in many ways, and clung to her toys. Castelos stared at her, trying to think of a way to say what he had to say without making her cry. For of all things in the world, only his daughter's tears could move the huge, brawling river god.

"My dear child," he said. "You may have wondered why I have been driving away those who would wish to marry you."

"I know you must have your reasons, father."

"Ah, you're a dutiful daughter, my pet. And I love you very much."

"But I must marry sometime, mustn't I father?"

"No, you must not."

"Really not?"

"Really."

"Never?"

"Never."

"Father . . . I may be about to cry."

"Please don't."

"But you're saying sad things. I don't care so much about having a husband, I don't think, but I have to have one to have babies, don't I? And I do want those. I've wanted a baby of my own ever since I stopped being one myself."

"Let me explain, my darling. And you'll see that I'm doing only what I have to."

She flowed to her feet, slid into his lap, and began to play with his beard. "All right, tell me," she whispered. Feeling even more keenly that he couldn't bear to hurt her, Castelos began to tell how he had offended the Hags of Fate and of the heavy curse they had laid upon him.

But he changed things a bit in the telling. He did not say that she, his daughter, was fated to bear three monsters but that the Hags had decreed that she would marry a monster who would do monstrous things to her.

"But father," she murmured, "he would have to love me to marry me, wouldn't he, so why would he want to do me harm?"

"A monster has a monstrous nature; it likes to hurt other creatures."

"Even his wife?"

"Maybe even especially his wife," replied the river god. "Only another monster can survive being married to one."

"Did those old hags tell you what he'd be like?"

"Not exactly, but I can assure you that all monsters are big and horribly ugly."

"Maybe not. Maybe it's mostly rumors. I've heard a lot of people say that you're a monster, daddy. But I, who know you best, see how kind and good you really are, even if you do sometimes change into other things and frighten people. So you see . . ."

"No, I don't see. What's all that have to do with anything? And if I'm so kind and good and you love me so much, why are you in such a hurry to leave me? No, don't cry! Please don't; I can't bear it. I'll tell you what. I'll go steal a baby somewhere. Maybe even a *couple* of brats. I'll bring them back here and you can take care of them. Will that do?"

"Think how sad their mothers will be if you steal them."

"Oh no, my sweet, dear, innocent child, not everyone's like you. Some of these poor peasants have more little ones than they can afford to feed. They'd be happy if someone took a few of them off their hands. If you like, I won't steal them; I'll buy them, pay more than they're worth. How's that?"

"Thank you, dear father, but I wouldn't know how to take care of their children. What would I do with them down here? I'd have to teach them to breathe underwater, and if I didn't do it right they'd drown."

"Children can learn anything if they start young enough. And if they drown, I'll get you some more."

"Oh, you're too good to me, and I do love you," said Calliroa. "But let me think about it a little."

"And you won't try to run off and get married in the meantime, will you?"

"I won't. I promise."

# 4

# The War God

Rumors spread through Thessaly and beyond of the ferocious river god and his beautiful naiad daughter. The news reached Mount Olympus, where the high gods dwelt, and came to the attention of Ares, Lord of Battles.

Now, Ares, like his father, Zeus, was interested in nymphs of every variety—naiad, dryad, Nereid—and when he wasn't making war, he was hunting them through the woodlands and waterways of the world. Nevertheless, his appetite for fighting was even greater. While he very much liked what he heard of the beautiful Calliroa, the idea of fighting her father intrigued him even more.

All the gods are big, but Ares was the biggest. In full armor he looked like a tower of bronze. The blade of his battle-ax was as large as a millstone. The shaft of his spear was an entire ash tree, trimmed. His spear point was longer than any ordinary sword. Eight black horses drew his enormous war chariot. They had been sired by Apollo's fire-maned stallions who drew the sun-chariot across the blue meadow of the sky. They were larger than elephants, and swifter than stags.

Ares happened to be between wars when he first heard of the river god's daughter, and he was eager for adventure. He leaped into his chariot and shouted "Go!" Ares never had to use a whip; his voice was enough. The stallions galloped down the slope of Mount Olympus, the great brass chariot trundling behind them, crushing rocks under its wheels. The horses thundered onto the wide Thessalian plain, then headed east by south toward a bend in the river where Castelos and Calliroa dwelt.

Sounds change as they pass through water, and the sounds now drifting down to the cave of Castelos were not muted but filtered, made musical. What the naiad heard was unlike anything she had ever heard before: a clanging as of a great gong being struck, again and again, growing louder as she listened. Her father had always warned her to remain in the cave when she heard strangers approaching, but this time she had to see for herself. Swiftly, before he could tell her not to, she slipped out of the cave and slid to the surface. She hid herself among the reeds along the shore and peeked out.

A great, dazzling shape swelled against the tree line. It was as if a piece of the sun itself had fallen and was rolling toward the river. There were horses; she heard bugling, heard someone shouting, but everything was lost in the huge brightness. The clangor grew louder and louder; it was like being inside a bell.

Calliroa squinted, trying to pierce the brightness. She saw a chariot, larger than any she had ever known, drawn by eight gigantic black stallions. They were rearing up at the riverbank, huffing and snorting. She saw a giant dismount and stride to the edge of the water. The sun bounced off his helmet, his breastplate, his greaves. He was a pillar of fire.

Calliroa knew that he had come for her and she was seized by terror. The very sight of him was too much to bear. He seemed to be crushing the life out of her, just standing there on the shore.

But the god didn't call for her; he called for her father. He put his huge, gauntleted hands to his mouth and bellowed. His voice seemed to roll off the hills, filling valley and plain: "River, river, give me your daughter! River, river, I want her now!"

Ares stood on the shore, waiting for the river god to answer his challenge. He was beginning to boil with the joyous rage he always felt before battle. He hoped that Castelos would not choose to yield his daughter peaceably but would fight for her.

Ares was not disappointed.

Out of the river rose Castelos in the first of his transformations: the giant snapping turtle. Like a living discus it spun toward the war god. The enormous creature skidded onto the bank, poked out its leathery head, and advanced. Ares laughed and struck with his spear haft, trying to smash the turtle's shell. To his amazement, it violated all rules of turtle behavior by leaping off the ground, catching the spear haft in its jaws, and snapping it in two.

But the war god's reflexes were incredibly fast; he actually thought with his body. He dropped his spear, shifted his grip, and swung his battle-ax. It struck the turtle and split its shell. He struck again with the flat of the ax. But the turtle scuttled free of its shell, and moving as swiftly as a lizard, slithered into the water, unharmed.

*The news reached Mount Olympus, where the high gods dwelt.*

Ares waded in after it, but stopped when he saw a gigantic sickle-fish rising to the surface. The war god was in a battle fever now, moving faster than his size would seem to allow. His bronze-gloved hand shot out, seized the curved horn blade that gave the sickle-fish its name, and whipped the fish up and down, smacking its body against the water. The horn snapped off. Ares took it up and flung it like a javelin, but missed, for the fish had already slid down into the depths.

Ares climbed back onto the riverbank and jeered, "Is that the best you can do, Castelos? Slimy little reptiles and freakish fish? Come on out and fight in your own form!"

But before he could finish his challenge, Ares found himself knee-deep in water. The river had begun to rise. Castelos had gone into his worst rage, which no one had ever survived. He was in flood.

Ares heard his stallions neighing. They were hock-deep in the rising water and could not gallop away because the massive chariot had begun to fill with water, making it too heavy to budge. Ares raised his ax and with one blow slashed the traces, freeing the horses. He leaped onto one of them, and the whole string galloped off toward high land. The river rolled in pursuit, bending trees, tossing huge boulders like pebbles, raging after the fleeing war god.

When the fighting had started, Calliroa had returned to the depths and hidden in the cave. Now, her father came to her and said, "He will be back, you know."

"But you defeated him, father. You chased him away."

"He will be back. Ares cannot allow himself to be defeated. He is the spirit of battle itself. He will call up his cousins, the Hundred-handed Giants. They will come over the mountains, every one of them carrying a boulder in each of his hundred hands. They will stand safely on the hills and hurl those boulders down upon me in a great shower of rocks. They will choke me. I shall not be able to flow; I shall be nothing but a heap of rocks along my entire length, and there shall I abide, dried up and useless underneath."

"Then," said Calliroa, "you must give me to him. Perhaps he will weary of me soon and let me come back to you."

"Never," said Castelos. "I will never give you to that raging brute. You must flee, my darling. Vanish. Hide. You are a water nymph; you have all the rivers and lakes and fountains of the world to hide in. So do so. Go now."

"But what about you, father? I can't leave you to be destroyed."

"Perhaps I won't be," replied the river god. "Perhaps when he learns that you have vanished he will forget about me. There are, after all, many nymphs to chase, many feuds to plant, many wars to wage. I'm only a little enemy in the scheme of things. But you must not tarry here. Go to sleep now. Refresh yourself for your journey. And by the first light of dawn, depart."

Calliroa flung herself, weeping, into his arms. Castelos stroked her face with his great, misty hand and cast her into a deep sleep.

Calliroa stood up in the river. The water came only to her hips. Tall and feeling taller, gleaming with wetness, she strode toward the little houses. A basket boat bobbed beside her. It floated into her shadow. Three faces stared up at her in amazement. She stooped swiftly, caught up the basket, and waded toward one of the little islands.

On reaching shore, Calliroa sat gently on the roof of the largest hut. The boatmen leaped out of the basket and perched on her wet shoulders. Others swung on her wet hair. She tumbled them into her lap and held them there. They tried to wriggle free, but she tickled them into submission.

One by one she turned the little people over in her hands, examining them carefully. They were pygmies but not potbellied or misshapen. She felt herself filling with strange, powerful joy as they squirmed in her grasp. Somehow, she had been granted

*Boats spread brown sails to catch the wind.*

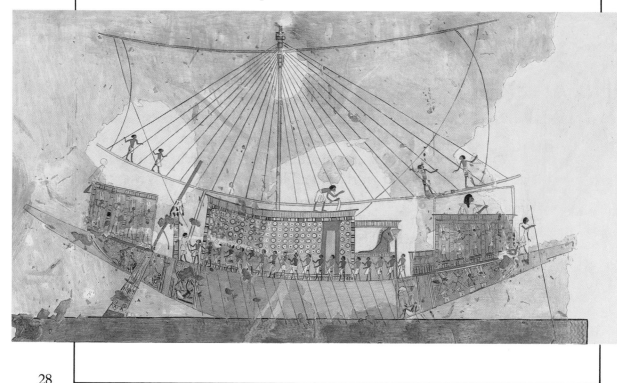

a villageful of living dolls to play with, not infants, but frisky adults, her own age and older.

They would be hers, these little people; she was the queen they had been waiting for since the beginning of time. She would live among them, defend them, rule them, reward and punish them, and be loved by them always.

Calliroa awoke in her father's cave under the river. But she was still in the grip of her dream; it hung its vapors about her as she prepared to leave. And, she realized, it was giving her a place to go.

She swam eastward down her father's river until it entered a gulf, then southward into the Middle Sea, and continued swimming southeast. Moving instinctively as a fish, she glided through those waters until she came to one hot shore where entered the wide, slow river of her dream. She swam upstream and discovered with joy that the vision sent to her was indeed a reality.

There, along the shore, ran a chain of islands. On one of the islands stood little houses. She saw tiny people launching basket boats. She rose from the water and waded toward them, and heard their thin voices crying out in welcome.

# 6

# A Vengeful Goddess

The tattle-bird was framed by nature for spying. It had eyes as sharp as a hawk's; no sound escaped it; and the underparts of its wings and body were the exact blue of the sky, allowing it to hover overhead without being seen. Hera, Queen of the Gods, who was always burning with curiosity about the activities of her fellow gods, employed a flock of these tattle-birds and rewarded them richly for their information. She had her gardener save the fattest worms for the birds, and forbade anyone to hunt them.

One perched now on Hera's shoulder. "Have you news for me, little bird?" the goddess asked.

"I do, I do," replied the bird. "You know the cranes and the pygmies of the Nile delta wage ceaseless war against one another."

"Do they now?" said Hera. "Well, that's an informative piece of natural history, no doubt, but I fail to see where it holds much interest for me. Have you no meatier news than that, little bird?"

"Patience, goddess, patience. I mention the cranes because it was one of them who told me what I am about to tell you. It

*Hera, Queen of the Gods, employed a*
*flock of tattle-birds and rewarded*
*them richly for their information.*

seems that the pygmies are now ruled by a naiad who arose from the river one day and made herself their queen. She's tall and beautiful, and they worship her."

"Worship?" said Hera coldly. "Worship is reserved for the gods."

"Exactly why I knew this would interest you," said the tattle-bird. "For the pygmies are saying that their queen is more beautiful and regal than any goddess, even you, O Hera."

"They do, do they? Well, when I get through with that Egyptian slut, nobody will be saying she's beautiful."

"She's not Egyptian. She's from Thessaly," said the bird.

"Thessaly? Then why is she in Egypt, playing around with those pygmies?"

"She fled there."

"Whom was she fleeing?"

"Well, this will interest you too. Her pursuer was your son, Ares."

"She spurned Ares?"

"She did. Her father defied your son. And the naiad fled all the way to Egypt, where she's been hiding ever since."

"Well, this works out nicely, doesn't it," said Hera. "I was going to send my Hundred-handed Giants to hold her prisoner there until I could figure out a suitable punishment. Now, I'll simply send Ares after her. Any close contact with him is punishment enough, especially after he's been rejected."

"Then you are satisfied with this tidbit I've picked up?"

"You've done well, little bird. Off with you to my gardener now, and he'll give you a spadeful of his fattest worms."

The tattle-bird flew away, and Hera sent for her son. But her messenger came back without him, reporting that Ares was on the other side of the world, igniting a war, a big one, big enough to keep him away for several months.

"Well," said Hera to herself. "What do I do now? Wait for Ares to return? In the meantime she'll be queening it over that scurvy mob of pygmies who call her goddess. This I cannot endure. I can't wait for Ares. I'll finish her off immediately. I'll send my giants now."

"Who has aroused your wrath *today*?" asked a creaking voice.

Hera whirled about. It was Atropos, the eldest Fate, who moved as softly as a spider when she wanted to. Hera was hot-

tempered and imperious. But no one ever refused to answer destiny's Hag.

"Tell me, lady," said Atropos. "Whom are you planning to finish off now?"

"An impudent naiad named Calliroa," replied Hera, "who rules over a tribe of Egyptian pygmies and dares to be worshiped as a goddess."

"I can see where that would enrage you. But allow me to ask you this. Whom do you hate more, Calliroa or Hercules?"

"Can there be any doubt?" answered Hera. "I intensely dislike this conceited water nymph, but I positively loathe Hercules, more than anyone else in the world!"

"Then you must restrain your wrath for the moment. Do not kill the naiad."

"Why not?"

"Because she is fated to produce a monster whom no one can kill, not even the hero, Hercules."

"Are you sure?"

"I am surety itself, my dear. As I decipher the tangled threads of destiny, this is what they seem to say: 'The monster that Calliroa will bear shall meet death at the hands of no one else.' "

"Very well," said Hera, "I shall refrain from killing her and shall welcome that monster when he makes his appearance. What is he to be called, by the way?"

"Geryon," said the Hag. "And you won't be disappointed in him."

Atropos then departed as silently as she had come.

"Nonetheless," said Hera to herself, "I can't let Calliroa go on sunning herself on that Egyptian islet, being adored by those damned pygmies. I won't kill her yet, but I'll put her somewhere where she'll be less admired, and a lot less comfortable."

Whereupon Hera sent for two of her Hundred-handed Giants and told them what to do.

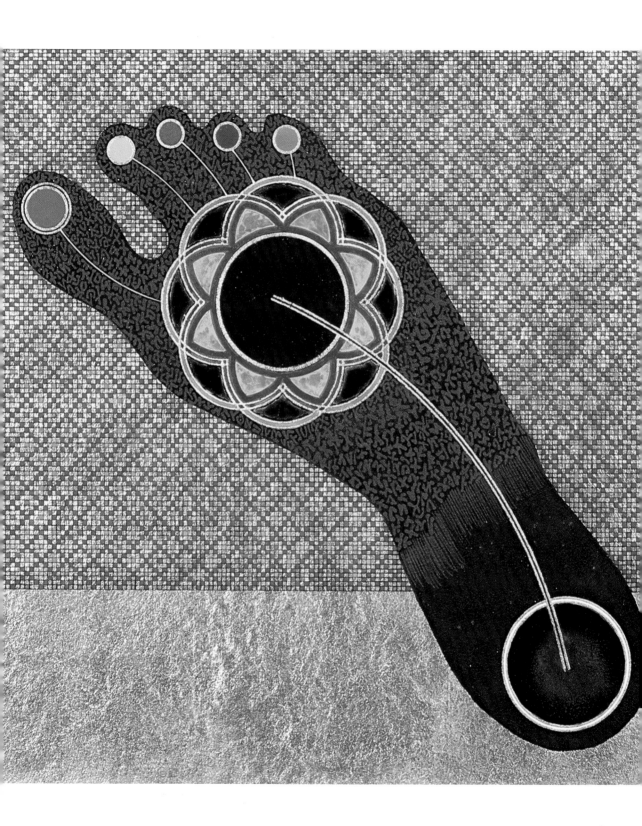

# 7

# Abduction

The pygmies were frantic. Their queen had disappeared. The night before she had bedded herself down as usual before the mud walls of the village. And, since her arrival, they had not bothered to post sentries at their gates. The naiad, they knew, was big enough and strong enough to drive away any marauding cranes. She had retired as usual the night before, and the village too had slept, only to awaken and find her gone.

There were no signs of struggle, there had been no cries for help, and they could find no trace of anything unusual except some big shallow dents in the mud, too long and wide to be footprints.

The pygmies were baffled. They hunted high and low. In their desperation they grew careless and sailed too far upstream in their basket boats. They were attacked by cranes and lost several of their best boatmen.

For days, the pygmies continued their search in vain. But their beloved queen was nowhere to be found. What they did not realize, of course, was that the trenches in the earth were indeed footprints left by the giants who had come in the night to seize the naiad. The pygmies were unable to imagine that any feet could be big enough to leave such prints.

"She'll come back one day," they reassured one another. "She appeared out of nowhere once, rising from the river mist, and she'll appear again as swiftly and magically as she did before."

So the pygmies waited, and waited, and swore to themselves they would wait forever.

The Hundred-handed Giants, obeying Hera, stole the naiad out of Egypt and bore her away to a punishment pen in Thrace, a land sacred to Ares.

This place did not look like a prison; at first sight it resembled a garden. But it was a garden that grew only two things—a jailer-vine that wrapped itself about anyone who tried to escape, and held the fugitive as securely as chains; and a punitive thornbush that could hobble about on its roots, striking with its thorny branches and flogging the vine-wrapped prisoner.

Calliroa saw one would-be escapee caught by the vine and flogged to bloody ribbons by the thornbush, and she was filled with terror. Nevertheless, she was determined to leave the garden, for Ares had returned from his latest war and was visiting her regularly now—and she loathed him.

Remembering her life with the devoted pygmies, she hated the huge, brutal Ares even more. She would try to escape, she resolved, and would risk being flogged to death. Calliroa devised a plan.

The next time Ares visited her, she dodged his embrace and raced away. He hurtled after her. She ran straight for the vine and almost into it, then swerved suddenly. Ares, closing upon her, charged into the jailer-vine, which immediately wrapped itself about the war god, binding him tight, weaving loop upon loop, so that the harder he struggled the more he entangled himself.

The thornbush, dutiful but without intelligence, hobbled over and began to flog Ares with its bramble whip. The naiad heard him bellowing with pain as she slipped out of the prison-garden and vanished among the trees.

Thenceforth, Calliroa lived in the woods like a dryad. Although longing for her father, she did not wish to go to him until she had borne the child she knew she was carrying. Some instinct directed her to seek solitude. She found a grove of trees and there gave birth.

When Calliroa saw what had been born to her she uttered a despairing shriek and fell into a swoon from which she did not awake for three days. Had the baby been an ordinary infant, it would have starved to death or been eaten by wild beasts. But it grew with monstrous speed, and by the end of the first day was able to crawl into the forest on its hands and knees. Since it had six hands and six knees, it scuttled along quite swiftly.

It, or they, were what might be called Siamese triplets, three complete bodies joined at the waist. The faces were bestial, with identical bulbous snouts, little pig eyes, and teeth so big their lips could not close.

Once in the forest this three-bodied monster, whom the Fates had named Geryon, began to hunt small game and caught enough to keep growing until he could hunt larger game.

As for Calliroa, she realized that the curse spoken by the offended Hags so long ago had finally ripened within her own body. Wracked by grief and self-loathing, she wandered from the grove where she had borne her terrible babe.

Geryon kept to the forest, teaching himself to hunt. He was able to kill small deer now, and to protect his kill from all but bear and lions. He was completely solitary, but living in triplicate, as it were, needed no other company. His solitude, nevertheless, was soon to be broken.

# 8

# The First Massacre

era had been keeping an eye on Geryon since his birth, several eyes in fact. She sent her tattle-birds to observe him and report on his progress.

Then, when Geryon was seven years old, Hera sent for him. She shuddered when the three-bodied child shambled into the palace on Olympus, but she controlled herself and spoke in a calm and friendly way.

"You are old enough now," she announced, "to start on your life's work."

"I know I'm a monster," said Geryon. "And I'm ready to start doing monstrous things."

"Very good. You shall go to Egypt immediately. Follow the Nile southward to where it flows around a chain of islands near its western bank. On one of these islands pygmies dwell. That place shall be your first killing ground. I want you to wipe out the entire settlement."

"Any particular way?" asked Geryon.

"Any that appeals to you. If there are too many to dispose of single-handed, you can always feed them to their enemies, the cranes. I'll expect you back here in two weeks' time with a full report on your activities. And I want to hear that the entire little pestilential nation has been wiped off the face of the earth."

"Thank you, your majesty. Farewell."

*The great birds dived, stabbing
their beaks into the bulging net
like wasps attacking rotten fruit.*

For the first few days, Geryon had good sport. He would cut off one pygmy from the rest, run him down, pluck him off the ground, and kill him with a chopping blow to the neck. Then he would stick the body into his bag, and set off after another. When he had taken five or six, he would skin them, spit them, and roast them over an open fire. All the exercise made him hungry.

After three days, however, Geryon wearied of pygmy flesh, and the little creatures were so easy to catch, and so helpless when caught, that hunting them was no longer any fun. So he decided to finish off the entire village in one stroke.

Wading into the river, he ripped a huge net from one of the moored fishing boats and dragged it in to shore. That night he crept up to the pygmy settlement and crouched in the darkness, watching the sentinels make their rounds. Geryon grunted, reached out with his six hands and strangled all six sentries; then he cast his net over the entire village.

He slung the net over his shoulder and bore the struggling, shrieking pygmies—men, women, and children—to a marsh where dwelt their enemies, the cranes. He had broken off a tree as he went, and was using it as a staff. Now he drove the staff into the mud, and hung the net from it; then he squatted in the brackish warm water, waiting for the cranes.

Finally he saw the great birds dipping toward him. They hovered briefly, then dived, stabbing their beaks into the bulging net like wasps attacking rotten fruit. He watched for a while, then left. Slogging away through the marshy ground, he heard the screams of the pygmies mingling with the cries of the hungry birds.

Back on Olympus, Hera praised him for the way he had handled his first assignment. Geryon listened expressionlessly, but he was pleased. It was his first massacre. It gave him a taste for murder which grew as he grew. And he was growing very fast.

# 9

## The River's Ally

alliroa returned to her father. He tried to kiss away her tears, but they flowed even faster.

"Why do you weep, my daughter?" Castelos asked.

"Oh father, I have given birth to a monster."

"Do not reproach yourself," he soothed. "Monsters may have very worthy parents. Think of Gaia, the great earth goddess, mother of us all. Did she not bear those primal monsters, the Cyclopes and the Hundred-handed Giants?"

"But Geryon is already full-grown!" cried Calliroa. "And he's a killer. He steals cattle and kills their owners if they resist, and even if they don't. Everywhere he goes, he leaves a wake of corpses in his path. And now, I know, he will come here, and carry out the vengeance of the Hags by slaughtering people on your shores, fouling your waters forever."

"Unless he's stopped," said Castelos.

"Who can stop him?"

"Do you know of Hercules?"

"The young hero? He's a son of Zeus, isn't he?"

"But not of his wife, Hera," said Castelos. "The jealous goddess hates Hercules and has condemned him to twelve labors. He has to fight the world's worst monsters. Hera's hope is that

*"Hercules has to fight the world's
worst monsters. Hera's hope is
that one of them will kill him."*

one of them will kill Hercules, but none of them have been able to, at least not yet."

"But father, what does he have to do with us?"

"I've asked him to challenge your son, Geryon."

"Will he be able to—with all those other monsters he has to fight?"

"I'm doing him a big favor in exchange." And the river god proceeded to tell his daughter about his meeting with Hercules.

Some days before, Castelos had recognized the young hero walking along his shore and had risen from the water in his own form.

"Greetings, Hercules," said Castelos.

"Greetings, whoever you are," answered Hercules.

"I am Castelos. I rule this river."

"I commend you, Castelos. Your stream is one of the most beautiful I have ever seen."

"I mean to keep it that way," said the river god. "But I need your help. I can help you in return."

"What do you mean?"

"I've heard about your next labor, which is to clean out the stables of Augeas."

"Yes," said Hercules. "That is my next task. And I would prefer to fight any monster you can name than to go within ten miles of that dung heap he calls a farm. Augeas is the supreme slob of the Western world. He keeps two hundred head of cattle tightly penned and hasn't mucked out the place in more than twenty years. There's policy behind all this. He craves his neighbors' property, but he is too lazy to steal; so he simply stinks them out and takes their acreage as they leave. Now the task set before me is to clean the stables in one day, leaving them spotless."

"And that's what I'm going to help you do," said Castelos.

"How?"

"I have a reputation for belligerence. I used to drive away my daughter's suitors by turning into other forms—snapping turtle, sickle-fish, whip-snake, and so on. When my enemy was especially strong I would strike as a flood. I would rise and rise, overflow my banks, and rage across the countryside. Now, I can do the same for you, not as an enemy, but as a friend. You shall appear to provoke me, just so we may deceive Hera, and I shall go into flood, hurl my waters after you across the fields, and follow you into the Augean valley. You will race across the barnyard, through the stables, and the waters will sluice through that filthy place, washing everything clean. The flood will then withdraw so swiftly that not a cow shall drown. Yes, I'll shrink back between my banks, and your task will be done."

"Why, that's brilliant!" cried Hercules. "I accept. Just one thing: give me a day to warn the people of the region so that they may retreat to higher ground."

*"You're ready for Hercules,
aren't you?" asked Hera. "You're
confident of overcoming him, I trus*

"Good," said the river
god. "I'll be ready whenever you
are."

"And what favor do you
seek in return?" asked Hercules.

"I am threatened by the
three-bodied monster, Geryon,
who happens by evil chance to
be my own grandson. Carrying
out a vengeful edict of the Fates,
he means to indulge in murder
along my shores, fouling my
water with blood and poisoning
me forever."

"And you want me to fight
Geryon—stop him, somehow?"

"Yes."

"It has been foretold that he can be killed by no one else.
You are aware of that, aren't you?"

"It will not be an easy task," said Castelos. "But none of
your tasks have been easy, have they?"

"Never mind, I'll try it," said Hercules. "It has already been
decreed that I combat Geryon and take back the cattle he has
stolen. Help me clean up the filthy stables, and I'll do what I can
against the three-bodied monster."

And that was our entire conversation," said Castelos to his
daughter. "I help him tomorrow. The very next day he will go
after Geryon."

Geryon sought Hera and found her in the Garden of the Gods
on the sunny slope of Mount Olympus. "Your friend Hercules
is after me," he told her.

"Indeed?" said Hera. "On his own? I meant you to be one of his labors—his last I hoped."

"Well, he seems to be planning this on his own. My dear grandfather, Castelos, has pleaded with Hercules to slay me before I fulfill the prophecy and turn his proud river into a foul, bloody trickle choked with corpses."

"You're ready for Hercules, aren't you?" asked Hera. "You're confident of overcoming him, I trust."

"Confident? The Nemean Lion was confident. And the Hydra too, no doubt. And they're both very dead."

"But the Fates have assured me that no one can kill you."

"Perhaps not. But there are no assurances that I can't be severely damaged."

"Geryon, is it possible that you're afraid of Hercules?" asked Hera.

"I don't know what fear is, majesty. No one ever taught me to be afraid. But I owe my string of victories not to obvious physical advantages but to the fact I weigh every detail before joining battle to make sure that I gain every possible advantage. In other words, goddess, I have begun to put together a plan of attack, and I want your help."

"Tell me what you need, and I'll do what I can," said Hera.

# 10

# Send A Storm!

bout ten miles off the eastern coast of Thessaly was an island that grew the most succulent grass in that part of the world. Here grazed sleek red cattle that were the envy of herdsmen everywhere.

This island had been ruled for many years by a kindly old man, known as the Old Drover, who was an expert in the ways of animals. One day Geryon had decided that the island would be a good place for him to live, at least for a while. He swam out to the island at night, climbed ashore, made his way to the palace, and slaughtered everyone in it—the Old Drover, his wife, his nine children, and his twenty-two grandchildren. Geryon spared only the servants, whom he meant to enslave and whom he threatened with death if they tried to escape.

Thereafter, Geryon dwelt on the island and increased his herds by a very simple method. He raided the mainland and robbed the coastal farms of their cattle, killing anyone who objected.

Hercules stood now upon a rocky beach on the eastern coast of Thessaly and stared over the sea, trying to make out the shore of Geryon's island in the gathering dusk. But it was too dark.

*Here grazed sleek red cattle that were the envy of herdsmen everywhere.*

He still had a decision to make—whether to wear his lion-skin armor and lion-head helmet. This gear could turn aside any blade and was therefore very useful in battle. But it made swimming difficult. And he preferred to swim to the island rather than use a boat because he wanted to slip ashore unseen and take Geryon by surprise.

"Well," he said to himself. "I'm too tired to swim now in any case. I'll go to sleep right here, and perhaps when morning comes I'll know what to do. Sleep sometimes confers wisdom."

Using the lion skin as a blanket against the night wind, Hercules curled up and fell asleep. He had no idea that he was being watched.

Hera stood on Olympus gazing down on the darkening coast. Next to her stood her brother Poseidon. The stormy-tempered god of the sea had always held a special affection for Hera and was always ready to do her a favor.

"See down there," said Hera. "That one, wrapped in a lion skin, sleeping on the headland?"

"I see him," said Poseidon. "Is he human? No, he can't be. Too big."

"That's Hercules," said Hera. "He's the one I loathe most in all the world, for he was spawned by my husband Zeus and his mother was the woman I despise beyond all others. In the morning Hercules means to swim to Geryon's island and challenge the monster."

"This Hercules has something of a reputation," said Poseidon. "But I should think Geryon would be able to handle him without too much trouble. Why, each of his three bodies is twice as big as Hercules. No one can stand up against such a beast."

"That may be. Nevertheless, Geryon himself has asked me to help him by crippling Hercules before the fight."

"How do you propose to go about that, dear sister?"

"By asking your help, dear brother."

"Ah, I thought this was no idle conversation. And how do you propose that I go about crippling that stalwart young fellow?"

"He lies now on that spit of land poking into your sea— the sea that you rule so absolutely, and can magnify or diminish at your will. This is what I want you to do. Whip up a storm. Send your waves rolling over that beach. Tear it off the mainland. Sweep it out to sea. Hercules will find himself on a patch of land that is rapidly shrinking. He will be forced to dive off and swim. When he dives, I want him to find himself among a school of hungry sharks, which you will have summoned."

"Hercules won't be easy prey, even for sharks," said the sea god.

"He can't possibly fight as well in the water as he does on land," said Hera. "At the very least they should be able to chew him up enough so that he won't be in any shape to fight a monster like Geryon. Will you do this, dearest brother, dearest friend?"

"Anything for you, my sister. I just hope it works out as well as you think."

# 11

# The Trial of Hercules

Hercules' lion-skin armor had been an unexpected bonus of his first great victory, slaying the Nemean lion. That lion had been considered invincible, and indeed had devoured everyone who dared to challenge it. It was large as an elephant with teeth like ivory daggers. Its claws were razor-sharp hooks, and its hide could not be pierced by sword, spear, or arrow.

After a great struggle, however, Hercules had managed to kill the beast, and had helped himself to its skin, which he first used as a weatherproof tent. Upon the occasion of his second labor, which was to kill the Hydra, he had decided to cut up the skin. A complete suit of armor was necessary to protect him, for Hydra poison was much more deadly than the strongest snake venom. So he had fashioned himself garments of lion's hide—rough trousers that covered the lower part of his body, a jacket with long sleeves, boots, and gauntlets. His helmet was the lion's head.

This armor immediately proved its worth. In his battle with the hundred-headed Hydra it had turned aside every one of a thousand vicious bites, and had enabled Hercules to slay his second monster.

Now, asleep upon the headland, Hercules was awakened by a terrible windstorm, which he had no way of knowing was aimed especially at him. He donned his armor. The lion skin kept him dry in the lashing rain, and its weight helped anchor him against the savage gusts. The rain turned to hail. Stones of ice pelted down at him. Any one of them could have shattered a man's skull, but they bounced harmlessly off the lion's head that was his helmet.

*Hercules watched the trees*
*sway . . . heard them crack. . . .*
*The moon swam in a rift of cloud.*

He watched the trees sway around him, heard them crack, saw them fall. The sea had risen so fast that it was impossible for him to race back over the neck of beach that led to the mainland. Waves were already dashing over it. Hercules was forced to stay where he was.

The headland where he had camped for the night was actually a low hill overlooking the sea. Then, suddenly, it was *at* sea. To please the vengeful Hera, Poseidon had packed three winds into a whirling cyclone and sent it spinning toward Hercules. It tore the spit of land away from the mainland and sent it scudding out into the ocean.

There was nothing Hercules could do. He planted himself there in his lion skin, trying to hold his footing and beginning to understand that such a storm was no freak of the weather but a god's spite—and he knew whose.

The wind dropped as suddenly as it had risen. The moon swam in a rift of cloud. Stars appeared. But the island was still rocking. He saw that the water was churning though there was no wind.

Then, something gigantic rose to the surface. Up, up it came—the huge glistening oval of a fish head—a fish of unbelievable size. It was a shark as big as a whale. It slid out of the water and towered above Hercules.

The terrible jaws gaped; the triple rows of teeth gleamed in the moonlight. Hercules retreated toward the center of his earth raft. The shark slid back into the water and began to circle him, whipping the surface to a froth.

Now, sharks—however large—can slip through the water without making a ripple if they wish. But this one was swimming untypically, and Hercules wondered why it was beating its tail and making such a froth. Then he realized that the churning water was making his island dwindle. Great clumps of soil were slipping off the edge and dissolving in the sea.

"This will never do," thought Hercules. "If the island goes and I end up in the water with that fellow, he'll have every advantage. I won't stand a chance. I don't exactly relish the prospect of meeting him out of the water, but it's definitely preferable. Of course, it would be best to get away from him completely. But how? Maybe I can move this patch of earth through the water and get back to the mainland. I can't have blown far."

Hercules picked up a fallen tree and swiftly broke off its smaller branches. He then took the entire tree to the edge of the water and began to use it as an oar, paddling what was left of his island back toward the mainland.

The water had become still. "Where's the shark?" he thought. "Have I lost him?" Then he knew he had not. His oar

snapped in his hand. The shark's jaws closed on the thick trunk and broke it as if it were a twig. Hercules hurled the stump of the tree at the shark and retreated hastily from the water's edge.

"This will get me exactly nowhere," he said to himself. "I'll have to fight the brute. But I'm determined not to fight him in the water."

Thereupon, he knelt and thrust his arm into the sea. That arm, of course, was encased in a lion-skin sleeve, and the hand

*Poseidon had packed three winds into a
whirling cyclone . . . . It tore the spit of land
away and sent it scudding out into the ocean.*

wore a gauntlet. He felt the great jaws close upon it. He had expected this. But he knew that the shark's teeth, sharp as they were, could not pierce his sleeve. What he had not counted on was the enormous strength of the jaws. While the teeth were unable to pierce through the lion skin, the jaws could crush. Hercules felt the incredible pressure on his arm; it was being crushed to jelly inside the armored sleeve.

He swelled his bicep and tried to will every small muscle—in arm, and wrist, and hand—to strain against the viselike grip. Bracing himself on his knees and exerting the last tatters of his strength, he swung his arm out of the water, pulling the shark with it.

With his other hand, encased in its lion-skin gauntlet, Hercules smashed at the shark's face. Struck again and again, great blows of the fist that had once knocked down a stone wall and then smashed the helmeted heads of the warriors hiding behind the wall. That fist was now pounding at the shark, breaking every bone in its rubbery head. Its eyes began to bleed. Its jaws slackened. It was dying. Hercules pulled his arm from the loose jaws, and swept the shark into the water. It turned belly up and floated away. Hercules picked up the tree that had been his oar and started paddling again, pushing his patch of earth, much shrunken now, toward a dark place looming upon the moonlit sea. It was an island, he knew, but he wasn't sure which one. This gulf was dotted with islands. He hoped it was not the one where Geryon dwelt. After fighting the shark, he felt he needed a few hours' sleep before meeting the three-bodied monster.

His clump of earth was dwindling rapidly now as Hercules poled it forward with mighty thrusts of the tree trunk. Finally, he reached shallow waters. But he didn't want to swim the remaining distance; there might be another gigantic shark lurking nearby.

Now he felt the last bit of earth crumbling under his feet. He flexed his knees and jumped off with all the power of his mighty thighs. The lion-skin armor was heavy upon him, and he carried spear and sword, bow and arrows. Nevertheless, he leaped through the air and skimmed over the offshore rocks, landing in the tidal pools.

Swiftly he waded onto the beach. Fatigue overwhelmed him. He sank to his knees. But he could not allow himself to stop here. The tide was coming in. With the last dregs of his will he forced himself to crawl up on the beach beyond the tide line and then fell into an exhausted sleep.

# 12

# Clam and Gull

ercules awoke at dawn, fully refreshed. For no matter how drained of strength he was, this son of Zeus could always replenish himself with a current of his father's energy, that magical voltage that branded the sky with blue lightning.

With strength restored, Hercules took stock of his surroundings. He had landed on a small islet, he saw. A hot, red tab of sun was pushing up over the eastern rim of the earth. It was going to be a brilliant summer day. Looking south, he saw another, larger island some miles away. As the sun climbed, he could see hills upon this island, low hills, thickly wooded, running down into grassy meadows and then to the sea.

Shapes moved upon the meadow; their slow, smooth pace and bulk told Hercules they were cattle. "That must be Geryon's island," he said to himself. "And those are his cattle grazing. But how am I to get there? I'm not going to swim. One giant shark is enough to last me for a while. My arm still feels half crushed. . . . But what strangeness is this? All creatures are magnified here, just as the shark was. Those birds up there; they fly like gulls, and their cry is a gull's cry, but they are larger than eagles!"

Indeed, every living creature was monstrously enlarged— for Hera had asked this of Poseidon and the sea god had done as she wished. Hercules was staring at a clam the size of a chariot wheel. The thing was alive, for it was spouting water and beginning to dig itself into the wet sand, sinking out of sight as he watched.

"Oh, no you don't!" cried Hercules. "I have need of you!"

He drew his sword and rushed at the clam. He pried open its shell, then studied what was inside. Hercules never killed any creature unnecessarily. Using his sword as delicately as a surgeon's scalpel, he swiftly severed the tendons, slid the blade under, and flipped the naked clam out of its shell.

"Sorry to evict you, my friend," said Hercules, "but I must borrow your dwelling place."

He watched the blob of phlegm that was the naked clam wobble toward the sea. A gull dived, screaming. But the clam slithered safely into the water.

"Yes," said Hercules. "I think my idea may work."

He lifted the two massive clamshells and carried them to the edge of the water. There he washed them out thoroughly and scrubbed them with sand, then rinsed them again. Finally, he climbed into one of the shells and closed the other over himself, pulling the two tightly together.

Something hard struck the shell, almost deafening him. But he had expected the shock and braced himself. He felt the shell rising, felt himself being lifted into the air. This is exactly what he had wanted. For gulls, he knew, loved clam meat but were able to break the shells open in only one way, by dropping them onto the rocks. He had noted that the incoming tide had covered the rocks of this islet, but that Geryon's shore was very rocky, girded by tall boulders whose tops poked above the swelling waters. And he had calculated that the only place a gull could break a clam was upon Geryon's shore.

Hercules lay curled in the darkness as he felt himself rushing through the air. "It's working!" he said to himself. "And I've assured myself safe passage, at least as far as the sharks are concerned. All I have to do now is survive the crash when the gull drops me. But it must be flying lower than usual; with me inside, this clam is very heavy." No sooner had he finished this thought, when he heard the gull scream and felt himself fall. The shell dropped heavily and shattered on the rocks.

Hercules did not rise but lay sprawled among the fragments of clamshell. The lion-skull helmet had protected his head; nevertheless, he had hit the rocks with such force that he was knocked unconscious.

He did not feel the gulls' claws striking his armor nor hear them scream as they quarreled over his body. For gulls are thievish. When one carries a clam over rocks, others will follow and dive after the falling shell, trying to snatch away the meat before its rightful owner can reach it.

It was only when he felt himself being tugged at that Hercules regained consciousness. But he immediately understood what was happening. The gulls, unable to pierce the lion skin, thought he was inside some sort of inner shell, and one of them was trying to lift him in order to drop him again.

Hercules clung to the rocks. His weapons had been knocked from his grasp in the fall, but he swung his fists, punched at the birds, and drove them off. One came at him from behind. He whirled just in time to seize the giant bird and wring its neck with one twist of his great gloved hands. When he flung the dead gull on the sand, the others dived at it in their cannibal way, forgetting him.

"Well, gulls," said Hercules. "I have repaid you poorly for wafting me safely over the shark-swarming seas, but you should not have returned to the attack."

He gathered his weapons and struck inland.

# 13

# Hero Meets Monster

ith the sun beating down hotly, Hercules felt himself basting in his armor. He stripped off the lion-skin garments and carried them. When he came to a hollow tree he hid the armor inside, marking the place in his mind so that he could find it again. Then, he passed through the wood onto a great meadow, and immediately wished he were back inside his armor.

Three enormous dogs were rushing toward him. He was still near the fringe of trees fortunately. With one powerful leap, he was among the lower boughs of an oak. Just in time. As he caught the bough he felt the hot breath of the dogs upon him. Mastiff they were, large as bull calves.

One after the other they leaped up, trying to catch any part of him in their great jaws. But Hercules was just out of their reach. He sat on the bough, considering them. "They're magnificent," he said to himself. "As splendid as the cattle they guard. Geryon certainly knows how to pick his animals. I'd hate to kill them. But I'm afraid they have no such reservations about me."

After pondering this for a while, Hercules drew an arrow from his quiver and studied it. "Pity to do this to a good arrow," he thought to himself, and snapped the sharp head off the shaft.

*One after the other the dogs*
*leaped up, trying to catch any*
*part of him in their great jaws.*

In those days, archers used short bows of yew or ash and drew the bowstrings only to their chests. But Hercules used a much longer bow made of antelope horn stiffened by copper wire. His arrows were as long as ordinary spears. And he drew the bowstring in a full-armed way, bending the bow almost in two, pulling the string back past his right shoulder. His arrows sped with deadly accuracy and with such force that, hitting a tree, they would bury themselves up to their feathers.

Now, however, he took the headless arrow and drew his bow only halfway. The blunted shaft traveled at half speed and struck one of the dogs in the rump, knocking it off its feet. It rolled on the ground, yelping in pain, then struggled up, and limped away.

Hercules broke the point off a second arrow and shot it in the same way, hitting the second dog squarely in the nose. This dog, too, rolled on the grass, yelping and whimpering, then scrambled away. Hercules did not have to shoot again. The third dog understood and raced off after his wounded companions.

Hercules waited until they were quite gone, then climbed down from the tree. The cattle, excited by the clamor of the dogs, milled about in a nearby meadow. Hercules decided to circle around the herd instead of passing through it. He still felt stiff and bruised and would have liked to loosen his muscles by wrestling a bull or two, but he also wanted to find Geryon's dwelling place as soon as possible.

He quickly ran over in his mind the things he had to do. "Observe his movements for a full day; study his habits; try to see how he handles himself in a fight—and finally, test that dismal prophecy. For if the prophecy is correct, and some magical mandate says that he cannot be killed, I shall have to avoid direct conflict and try to devise some other way to cope with the monster."

Hercules made his way through the woods until he entered a clearing and knew immediately that he had found Geryon's dwelling place. At first sight, it resembled a cave more than a house, for it was built of huge boulders. It looked like the most ancient of habitations, built in the very dawn of time.

A huge grass sward fronted the dwelling. Hercules saw that Geryon preferred to dine outside. His table was a slab of stone resting on four tree stumps. He saw smoke arising from behind the house, and smelled the savor of meat roasting.

Then he saw something huge shambling out of the stone hovel. Despite all his experience of monsters, Hercules gaped in dismay. For this—or these—appeared more fearsome than anything he had encountered before. Each of the three bodies was twice as tall and at least twice as wide as his own.

Hercules watched the monster very closely as it shuffled toward the table. Although Geryon was actually three separate entities bound together at the waist, he still managed to move with absolute coordination, as if one brain were directing all the action. Nevertheless, Hercules noted, the two side bodies could do two entirely different things at once, while the middle body was pursuing a third activity—and they did not interfere with one another, or betray the least awkwardness. And when they had to move in concert, the separate activities flowed smoothly into a single set of movements.

All this told Hercules that if it ever came to close combat, he would have a most difficult time.

Geryon was seated now. Servants were crossing the grass, bearing trays of food. Hercules had watched greedy creatures before—huge ones that devoured everything in sight—but he had never witnessed gluttony like Geryon's. Every two hours, three cooks and their helpers laid out three different meals on the table. For each body had its own favorite food. The right-hand body craved pork. The middle body liked mutton. And the body on the left preferred goat meat.

"Odd that he doesn't like beef," thought Hercules. "No one on earth has such fine herds. Perhaps he doesn't want to eat his own cattle."

One of the servants, setting a haunch of mutton on the table, was unfortunate enough to splatter his master with a bit of gravy. Without rising from his seat, Geryon shot out one of his six hands, caught the man about the neck, and squeezed until the servant's face grew purple and his eyes bulged. Then the hand dropped the dead body to the grass. And not one of the three monster's mouths had ceased chewing for a second.

"I don't want to believe that this ogre can't be killed," thought Hercules. "I shall have to test the prophecy myself."

He withdrew into the woods to try his arm and sharpen his aim. He raised his spear and flung it at an oak. The spear passed entirely through the thick bole, splitting it as cleanly as the ax of a woodsman splitting a log. Retrieving his spear, he loped back toward Geryon's house.

The monster was still at the table. His three heads were sprawled on the stone slab; he was asleep, snoring hoarsely. Hercules came closer and hurled his spear with all his force. It cleaved the bright air, then slowed strangely, without dropping, as if the air had suddenly jelled around it. Hercules saw that the air about

Geryon's sleeping heads had indeed thickened to a murk. The spear point stopped one inch from the monster's middle head.

The murk cleared; the aspic air faded. The spear dropped to the grass, and all eyes remained shut. "The prophecy does not lie," thought Hercules. "Some demonic destiny shields him from death."

He walked back into the shade of the trees. He needed to think. "What I've learned about prophecies," he continued, "is that they don't always mean exactly what they say. Fate often speaks in code. Now what does this prophecy say precisely? 'Geryon can't be killed'. . . . No, that's not it. It's longer than that. 'Geryon can't be killed by anyone'. . . . That's not right either. 'Geryon can be killed by no one else.' That's it. No one *else*. What does 'else' mean? It means another being, another creature, not himself. Himself? But he's three selves. Hmm. . . . There's the seed of an idea in there somewhere."

Hercules went deeper into the woods, then climbed a hill. He spotted a goat and chased it, springing from boulder to boulder

*Hercules went deeper into the woods.*

as the animal leaped ahead of him. He cornered it finally in a cleft of rock. It turned and charged him, lowering its big, curved horns, trying to butt him off the hill.

Hercules caught one horn in each hand, swung the goat off the ground, slung it over his shoulder, and carried it down the hill to a place where three paths came together. There he tethered it to a tree and set off into the woods again. He was after wild boar now.

First he returned to the hollow tree where he had hidden his armor, and dug out his lion-skin gauntlets. For a boar is very dangerous to hunt. It is built low to the ground, is one slab of muscle, and moves very fast. Its tusks are deadly weapons. When cornered, it turns and charges.

Now a huge one burst out of the underbrush. As soon as it spotted Hercules, it lowered its head and charged. Hercules reached out his gauntleted hands. Seizing the boar by its tusks, he arose, swinging the beast high and smashing it to the ground, knocking its wind out. It seemed ten times as heavy as the goat when he heaved it onto his shoulders and carried it back to the hill. There he tethered the boar to a tree near where he had tied the goat and ran down the path again to find a sheep.

He came upon a meadow where sheep were grazing, and chose a big ram. Despite its horns, the animal was no fighter.

Hercules simply lifted it upon his back and carried it to where he had tethered the other animals, feeling quite weary by the time he had it tied to a third tree. But he could not permit fatigue; he had much to do before he could sleep.

He returned to the clearing and stood in the dappled shade of the trees near the house so that he could see without being seen. Geryon was still at the table, but awake now, bawling for food. Hercules saw the servants beginning to file out from behind the house.

He raced across the grass, pulled a tray out of the hands of an amazed cook, and carried it toward the table. Standing behind Geryon, he held the tray over him and calmly turned it upside down.

A ten-pound ham hit the middle head. A gallon of hot gravy splashed over the two other heads. Hercules moved around to the front of the table so that the monster could see who had done this to him, then began to run. Geryon sprang after him.

For all the monster's bulk, he was extremely fast. Running on six legs, he could outrace a good horse. But Hercules easily kept ahead of him, holding the same distance between them— speeding up and pulling ahead when the monster came too close, lagging again when he thought they were too far apart.

Geryon would have kept chasing him in any case. The three-bodied monster was in a flaming rage now, not only because he had been assaulted in that unbelievable way but also because he had been running so long. He had missed a meal and was about to miss another. Hunger mixed with rage and clawed at his bellies.

*He came upon a meadow where sheep were grazing, and chose a big ram.*

Geryon saw that he could not catch the young man. He scooped up a rock as he ran and hurled it. His aim was good. The rock struck Hercules in the calf. It would have shattered the leg bone of any other man, but Hercules' bones were like iron rods. His flesh, though, could be bruised and his muscles torn. And the stone did wound him.

His leg hurt terribly; the pain slowed him down. Geryon put on a burst of speed and was gaining on Hercules, who angled off now, left the road, and ran across a patch of woodland, leaping over fallen logs. Hercules chose this rough route because he thought that, despite his injured leg, he would be able to out-jump Geryon.

It was true. Forcing himself to ignore the agonizing pain of his leg, he soared over the tangle of fallen trees, while Geryon had to clamber over them. Hercules was able to draw ahead slightly, but he was terribly weary now. He had hunted all day without food or rest, while Geryon had eaten and slept. He knew that he would have to end this chase soon or Geryon would catch up with him and break him to pieces with those six monstrous hands.

Hercules was running uphill now. He swerved and headed for a stream that was tumbling down the slope. He ran straight toward the water, then leaped. He sailed over, landed on the other side, and kept running. Geryon jumped also, but he came down in the middle of the stream and stumbled, trying to regain his footing. He plowed through the water and climbed out onto the other bank.

But now Hercules was well ahead, and racing to where he had tethered the animals. He drew his knife as he ran. When he reached the goat, he slashed its rope, setting the animal free. Raced to the tree where the pig was tied, and cut that rope. Sped to the third tree, and cut the rope that bound the sheep.

But he didn't let them run free. With his last strength Hercules caught them in his arms. He hurled the boar to the left, the goat to the right, and the sheep straight ahead.

The three bodies of Geryon, hurtling toward their enemy, saw food fleeing before them — the favorite food of each body racing away. These bodies were raging with hunger. They were used to eating every two hours and had now missed three meals.

The right-hand body tried to go after the pig; the left-hand body tried to wrench itself away to follow the goat. And the middle body forged ahead after the ram. With three bodies trying to go in three different directions, they went nowhere. They were glued to the spot.

*When he reached the goat,*
*Hercules slashed its rope, setting the animal free.*

*The right-hand body tried to go after the pig;
the left-hand body tried to wrench itself away
to follow the goat . . . but they went nowhere.*

They shook violently, trying to tear free. But the more they tried, the less they could move. Six legs began kicking at one another. Six hands became six fists, pounding at the nearest face. Three sets of teeth tore at each other's shoulders and necks.

Hercules, hiding from behind a tree, watched the three bodies of the giant fight among themselves—doing to Geryon what no one else could do. They broke each other's face bones, kicked each other's legs to a pulp, clawed and butted. Blood bubbled when mouths tried to scream. Geryon fell. He looked like a crab crushed by a rock.

Hercules stood over him and saw that his enemy was dead. "That was it, then," he said. "That was the joker in the prophecy:

This monster could be killed by no one *else*. But, torn by conflicting hungers, his selves hating one another, he went to war with himself, destroyed himself. And I'm glad I was able to help."

There was one more thing Hercules had to do. He rounded up Geryon's herds and, aided by mastiffs, drove them down to the sea. The recent storm had felled many trees, and Hercules labored mightily for an entire day, hauling the great trunks down to the beach and lashing them together into gigantic rafts.

He then bound raft to raft, making a long line of barges, and drove the cattle on board. Planting himself on the first raft, he used a tree trunk to paddle the entire string of barges, loaded with cattle, across the strait to the mainland.

Word of Hercules' victory had reached the coastal villages of Thessaly, and a great crowd had come down to the beach to welcome him. Hercules unloaded the herd from the rafts and thanked the people for coming to greet him. He bade those who had been robbed by Geryon to reclaim their cattle.

Hercules was very tired, but happy. He had no way of knowing that the Hags of Fate were hovering above him, for they had made themselves invisible.

"Never mind, sisters," hissed Atropos. "Hercules has tangled our threads and thwarted a doom and gone to a great deal of trouble to preserve the purity of one stupid river. But patiently, patiently, we spin our webs—slowly, patiently, preparing so terrible a death for Hercules that it will be spoken of forever, and strike the fear of Fate into all the generations to come."

# Acknowledgments

Letter Cap Illustrations by Hrana L. Janto

Opposite page 1, THE FURY, *drawing by Michelangelo (1475–1564)*
  Courtesy of the Uffizi Gallery, Florence
    Photo: Bildarchiv Foto Marburg/Art Resource, New York

Page 3, ANCESTRAL WORSHIP *(1947) by Theodoros Stamos; gouache, ink, and pastel on paper (17 1/2" × 23 3/8")*
  Courtesy of the Collection of Whitney Museum of American Art, New York; purchase (Acq. No. 48.9)
    Photo: Geoffrey Clements, New York

Page 4, DARK WING STORM *(1985) by Emilio Cruz, oil on canvas (7' × 7')*
  Courtesy of the Anita Shapolsky Gallery, New York

Page 7, THE COMING OF SPRING *by Charles Burchfield (1893–1967), watercolor on paper mounted to presswood (34" × 48")*
  Courtesy of The Metropolitan Museum of Art, New York; George A. Hearn Fund, 1943 (43.159.6)

Page 8, NIGHT SWIM *(1986) by Dea Cleavanger, acrylic on canvas (38" × 58"), from the "Sirens" series*
  Courtesy of the Helio Galleries, New York

Page 10, BY THE POND *(ca. 1912) by Kenneth Hayes Miller, oil on composition board (16 1/2" × 11 1/2")*
  Courtesy of the Collection of Whitney Museum of American Art, New York; gift of Mrs. Grant Sanger (Acq. No. 55.16)
    Photo: Geoffrey Clements, New York

Page 12, FIGURE AND POOL *by John Singer Sargent (1856–1925), watercolor on paper (13 3/4" × 21")*
  Courtesy of The Metropolitan Museum of Art, New York; gift of Mrs. Francis Ormond, 1950 (50.130.62)

Page 15, ICARIAN BAPTISM *(1986) by Simon Carr, oil on canvas (7' × 7')*
  Courtesy of the Bowery Gallery, New York

Page 16, STUDIES OF A RIVER GOD *by Peter Paul Rubens (1577–1640), black chalk on green buff paper (16 1/4" × 9 7/16")*
Courtesy of The Museum of Fine Arts, Boston; Frances Draper Colburn Fund (20.813)

Page 20, ALL YOU ZOMBIES (TRUTH BEFORE GOD) *(1986) by Robert Longo, cast bronze, mechanized steel pedestal, charcoal and graphite on canvas (176 1/2" × 195" × 177 1/2")*
Courtesy of Metro Pictures, New York
Photo: Bill Jacobson Studio

Page 23, FEAST OF THE GODS *by C. V. Poelenberg (1586–1667), oil on canvas*
Courtesy of Kunstmuseum, Basel
Photo: Kavaler/Art Resource, New York

Page 26, NOFRETARI KNEELING IN ADORATION, *copy of a wall painting from the Tomb of Nofretari, Valley of the Queens (1290–1223 B.C.)*
Courtesy of the Egyptian Expedition of The Metropolitan Museum of Art, New York; Rogers Fund, 1930 (30.4.144)

Page 28, STATE SHIP OF HUY PREPARING TO SAIL UP THE NILE *(ca. 1360 B.C.) copy (top) of a wall painting from the Tomb of Huy, Viceroy of Nubia under Tutankhamen*
Courtesy of the Egyptian Expedition of The Metropolitan Museum of Art, New York; Rogers Fund, 1930 (30.4.19)

Page 30, STATUE OF A GODDESS WITH A BIRD, *Greco-Roman terra cotta*
Courtesy of the National Museum of Archaeology, Reggio Calabria
Photo: Scala/Art Resource, New York

Page 32, CRY OF THE JUKE BOX *(1951–52) by Martha Visser't Hooft, oil on canvas (48" × 34")*
Courtesy of the Collection of Whitney Museum of American Art, New York; purchase, with funds from the Wildenstein Benefit Purchase Fund (Acq. No. 53.7)
Photo: Geoffrey Clements, New York

Page 34, THE FURY *by Edward R. Thaxter (1854–1881), marble (h. 26")*
Courtesy of The Museum of Fine Arts, Boston; William E. Nickerson Fund (63.5)

Page 36, FOOT *(1984) by Bernard Maisner, gold leaf, egg tempera, and acrylic (10' × 10')*
Courtesy of the Collection of Janet Liles and Andre Georges

Page 40, JANUS DUPLEX *(1985) by Emilio Cruz, oil on canvas (6' × 5')*
Courtesy of the Anita Shapolsky Gallery, New York

Page 42, YOU *(1951) by Irene Rice Pereira, outer surface: metal leaf and mixed media on glass; inner surface: metal leaf and tempera on wood (30" × 23")*
Courtesy of the Collection of Whitney Museum of American Art, New York; purchase, with funds from anonymous foundation (Acq. No. 62.47)

Page 44, AUTUMN LANDSCAPE *designed by Louis Comfort Tiffany (1848–1933), stained glass window (11' × 8 1/2')*
Courtesy of The Metropolitan Museum of Art, New York; gift of Robert W. de Forest, 1925 (25.173)

Page 46, HERCULES FIGHTING CERBERUS *(ca. 1520) majolica ware plate from Italy*
Courtesy of The Metropolitan Museum of Art, New York; Robert Lehmann Collection, 1975 (1975.1.1082)

Page 48, HEAD OF A WOMAN *by Pablo Picasso (1881–1973), linoleum cut, one block printed in black, green, red, and yellow on Arches paper, edition of 50 (image 25 1/4" × 20 7/8")*

Courtesy of The Metropolitan Museum of Art, New York; the Mr. and Mrs. Charles Kramer Collection, gift of Mr. and Mrs. Charles Kramer, 1979 (1979.620.57)

Page 50, MARINE: THE WATERSPOUT *by Jean Desire Gustave Courbet (1819–1877), oil on canvas (27 1/8" × 39 1/4")*
Courtesy of The Metropolitan Museum of Art, New York; gift of Horace Havemeyer, 1929, the H. O. Havemeyer Collection (29.160.35)

Page 52, BRONZE BULL *statuette from Arabia (6th century B.C.)*
Courtesy of The Metropolitan Museum of Art, New York; Rogers Fund, 1947 (47.100.85)

Page 54, HERCULES *(ca. 500 B.C.) Etruscan bowl*
Courtesy of the Vatican, Museo Gregoria Etrusco
Photo: Scala/Art Resource, New York

Page 56, MOONSCAPE *(1985) by Gary Mayer, oil on canvas (48" × 60")*
Courtesy of the Feigenson Gallery, Detroit

Page 58–59, ISLANDS OF MATSUSHIMA *by Ogata Korin (1658–1716), six-panel folding screen, ink and colors on paper (155 × 65 cm.)*
Courtesy of The Museum of Fine Arts, Boston; Fenollosa-Weld Collection (11.4584)

Page 62, SEA GULLS, GASPE *by Milton Avery (1885–1965)*
Courtesy of the Addison Gallery of American Art, Phillips Academy, Andover, Massachusetts

Page 66, CHIEF'S HEADDRESS MASK *made by the Niska Indians, British Columbia*
Courtesy of The Museum of the American Indian, New York (No. 3370)

Page 68, UNTITLED *(ca. 1986) pastel on paper by Barbara Quinn*
Courtesy of Barbara Quinn, New York

Page 71, THE FOREST IN WINTER AT SUNSET *by Pierre Etienne Theodore Rousseau (1812–1867), oil on canvas (64" × 102 3/8")*
Courtesy of The Metropolitan Museum of Art, New York; gift of P. A. B. Widener, 1911 (11.4)

Page 72, HERCULES AND THE ERYMANTHIAN BOAR, *Italian bronze statuette (17th century), after a model by Giovanni Bologna (h. 17 1/2")*
Courtesy of The Metropolitan Museum of Art, New York; the Jack and Belle Linsky Collection, 1982 (1982.60.100)

Page 73, MOUNTAIN SHEEP, *prehistoric petroglyph, Inyo County, California*
Courtesy of The Museum of the American Indian, New York (No. 4134)

Page 75, RED GOAT *(1983) by John Alexander, oil on canvas (74" × 84")*
Courtesy of The Metropolitan Museum of Art, New York; the Emily and Jerry Spiegel Collection, purchase, Jerry Spiegel Foundation, Inc. gift, 1983 (1983.256)

Page 76, AGROPHOBIA *(1986) by Emilio Cruz, oil on canvas (6' × 8')*
Courtesy of the Anita Shapolsky Gallery, New York

# BOOKS BY BERNARD EVSLIN

Merchants of Venus
Heroes, Gods and Monsters of the Greek Myths
Greeks Bearing Gifts: The Epics of Achilles and Ulysses
The Dolphin Rider
Gods, Demigods and Demons
The Green Hero
Heraclea
Signs & Wonders: Tales of the Old Testament
Hercules
Jason and the Argonauts